D1502057

# Looking at . . . Muttaburrasaurus

## A Dinosaur from the CRETACEOUS Period

**Weekly Reader**
**BOOKS**

Published by arrangement with Gareth Stevens, Inc.
Newfield Publications is a federally registered trademark
of Newfield Publications, Inc. Weekly Reader is a federally
registered trademark of Weekly Reader Corporation.

Library of Congress Cataloging-in-Publication Data available upon request from publisher.
Fax: (414) 225-0377 for the attention of the Publishing Records Department.

ISBN 0-8368-1346-4

This North American edition first published in 1995 by
**Gareth Stevens Publishing**
1555 North RiverCenter Drive, Suite 201
Milwaukee, Wisconsin 53212 USA

This U.S. edition © 1995 by Gareth Stevens, Inc. Created with original © 1995 by Quartz
Editorial Services, Premier House, 112 Station Road, Edgware HA8 7AQ U.K.

Consultant: Dr. David Norman, Director of the Sedgwick Museum of Geology,
University of Cambridge, England.

Additional artwork by Clare Herronneau.

Printed in the United States of America

**Weekly Reader Books Presents**

# Looking at . . . Muttaburrasaurus

## A Dinosaur from the CRETACEOUS Period

by Tamara Green

Illustrated by Tony Gibbons

THE NEW
DINOSAUR
COLLECTION

Gareth Stevens Publishing
**MILWAUKEE**

# Contents

# Introducing
# Muttaburrasaurus

First discovered in 1981 in Australia, **Muttaburrasaurus** (<u>MUT</u>-A-<u>BUR</u>-A-<u>SAW</u>-RUS) was a large, plant-eating dinosaur that lived about 100 million years ago.

Remains of **Muttaburrasaurus** have not been found anywhere

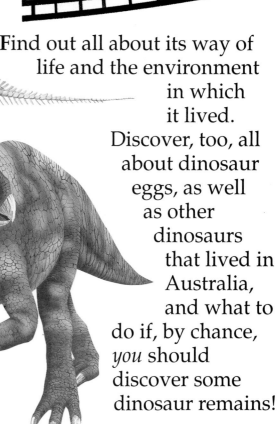

Find out all about its way of life and the environment in which it lived. Discover, too, all about dinosaur eggs, as well as other dinosaurs that lived in Australia, and what to do if, by chance, *you* should discover some dinosaur remains!

else in the world. So scientists wonder whether it lived only in this part of the Southern Hemisphere.

You'll come face-to-face with this strange-looking creature from prehistoric times as you turn the pages of this book.

5

# Australian dinosaur

About 23 feet (7 meters) long, **Muttaburrasaurus** was twice the height of today's average adult human being when the dinosaur stood on all fours. It was a lot taller than you.

**Muttaburrasaurus** was named after the place in Australia where it was found — Muttaburra, in the state of Queensland.

It generally walked around on its two back legs. But it could also get down on all fours when it wanted to feed on low-lying plants.

Most experts believe **Muttaburrasaurus** was a herbivore — that is, a vegetarian, living on plants only. But a few scientists also believe this dinosaur may have eaten meat at times.

This may have been difficult, though, with a toothless beak and teeth just at the sides of its mouth.

Although scientists have not found the complete remains of this dinosaur, they are fairly certain it had a nasty thumb spike. It used this as a weapon for self-defense, just as **Iguanodon** (IG-WA-NO-DON) did. They think this is the case because it is like **Iguanodon** in so many other ways. This spike may also have been useful for reaching high branches when feeding on tall trees.

And just look at that large, flat head with the prominent arch over its snout! It certainly seems to have been a handsome prehistoric beast!

# The inside story

When scientists discover remains, they hardly ever succeed in digging up a complete skeleton. They often have to guess from what they find how the whole creature must have looked when it roamed Earth all those millions of years ago.

From this drawing of its skeleton, you can see that **Muttaburrasaurus** was a strongly built creature. It also had a flexible neck. Being able to move its neck easily would have helped it find food and spot enemies.

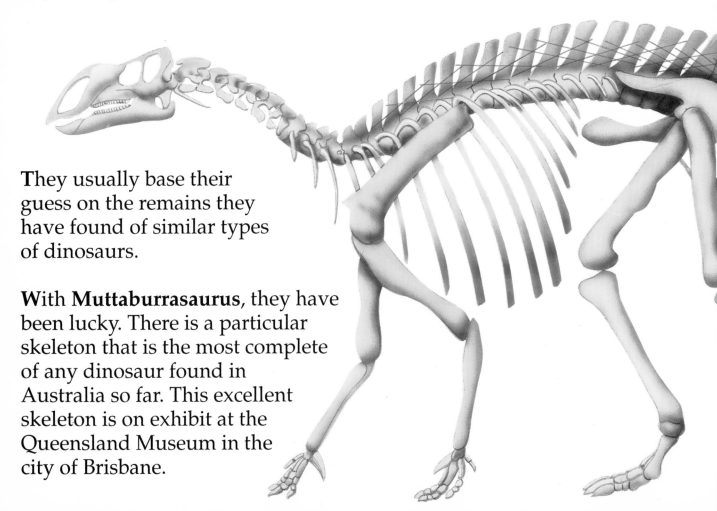

They usually base their guess on the remains they have found of similar types of dinosaurs.

With **Muttaburrasaurus**, they have been lucky. There is a particular skeleton that is the most complete of any dinosaur found in Australia so far. This excellent skeleton is on exhibit at the Queensland Museum in the city of Brisbane.

Its back legs, as you can see, were quite thick, while its arms were shorter. It would probably have reared up on these powerful back legs either to reach for high-growing plants or to see for a long distance. But it could also walk on all four limbs.

Take a look now at the spiked thumbs on the front limbs of **Muttaburrasaurus**'s skeleton, as shown in this drawing. These spikes have not actually been found. But **Muttaburrasaurus** is

If you study **Muttaburrasaurus**'s skull for a moment, you will see a prominent bump over its nostrils. No one is sure what it was for. It may have helped protect its head from attack. Or perhaps the size of the bump helped males or females recognize each other.

You can see, too, that it had no teeth at the front of its mouth — only in its cheeks. The snout was long and narrow.

Notice now how the bones in **Muttaburrasaurus**'s tail gradually decrease in size toward the end.

There were, of course, no humans as yet in **Muttaburrasaurus**'s time.

so like **Iguanodon** in other ways that scientists think it, too, must have had spiked thumbs for use as weapons. So they have reconstructed it with these.

But, on the whole, if you had been able to meet one, how friendly do you think it might have been? Would you have had to run for your life, or would you have dared to offer it a few branches?

# Muttaburrasaurus

In 1963, a rancher working in Muttaburra, central Queensland, Australia, contacted the Queensland Museum in great excitement.

On the banks of the Thomson River, where his cattle grazed, he had been amazed to find what looked like the remains of a dinosaur!

The cattle had obviously been curious about it, too, and had scattered the bones.

Worse, before a dig could be organized, people living nearby had taken some of the fossils as souvenirs.

# discovered

Once the local population heard how important the find was, however, they returned much of what had been taken.

It was good that they did, or experts might never have been able to piece together the remains of this prehistoric creature.

Scientists later named the unique specimen **Muttaburrasaurus langdoni** after the place where it had been found and also the rancher, whose surname was Langdon, who first discovered and reported it.

# Fighting back

It was a warm, quiet Cretaceous afternoon in the depths of what is now Queensland, Australia. A young, lone **Muttaburrasaurus** had found an appetizing clump of weeds by the marshes and was chomping away, enjoying a tasty treat and oblivious to the rest of the prehistoric world.

They circled the **Muttaburrasaurus** as if in warning. The dinosaur, however, was too deeply engrossed in its meal to pay attention.

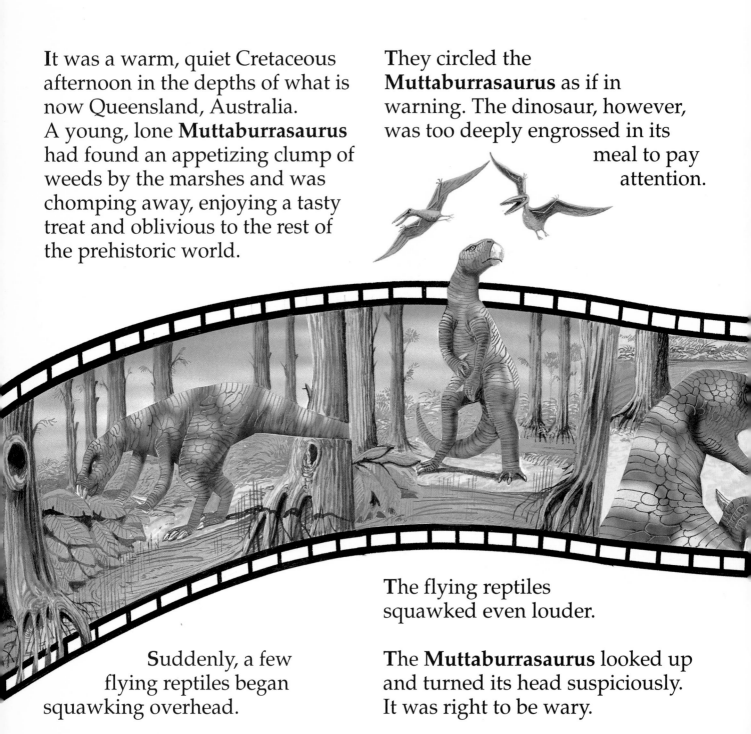

The flying reptiles squawked even louder.

Suddenly, a few flying reptiles began squawking overhead.

The **Muttaburrasaurus** looked up and turned its head suspiciously. It was right to be wary.

There could be enemies around — dangerous flesh-eaters, for instance — that would fight to the death for a chance to eat delicious **Muttaburrasaurus** meat.

The **Muttaburrasaurus** saw nothing to worry about. Yet the flying reptiles were now making even louder noises. The dinosaur responded by sniffing at the air. Just as it caught the scent of approaching meat-eaters, the predators appeared.

They snarled ferociously, opening their huge jaws in one dreadful, threatening gesture. It seemed the **Muttaburrasaurus** would hardly stand a chance. But it had its nasty thumb spikes for protection. As the carnivores leapt, the dinosaur stabbed with both spikes simultaneously. The beasts howled in pain. Now the **Muttaburrasaurus** was quick to see its opportunity.

The **Kakuru** (KAK-OO-ROO) leapt out from behind a group of tall trees where they had been lurking.

It ran off speedily to rejoin its family group. **Muttaburrasaurus** had been saved by the pterosaurs' warning and its own handy thumb spikes!

# Dinosaur eggs

Some of the world's largest auction houses have recently sold several remarkable dinosaur eggs that are millions of years old. A great many of these eggs have been exported illegally from China and Mongolia where several have been found. They have been bought not only by museums around the world, but also by individual collectors who think their value will rise.

The first dinosaur eggs to be found belonged to **Protoceratops** (PRO-TOE-SER-A-TOPS), a dinosaur living in what is now Mongolia's Gobi Desert. Most were found in clutches within scooped-out nests containing twelve or more unhatched eggs. They were many times bigger than a chicken's egg.

Scientists have now tried to x-ray some eggs, using special techniques, to see if there could be traces of baby dinosaurs that were developing inside.

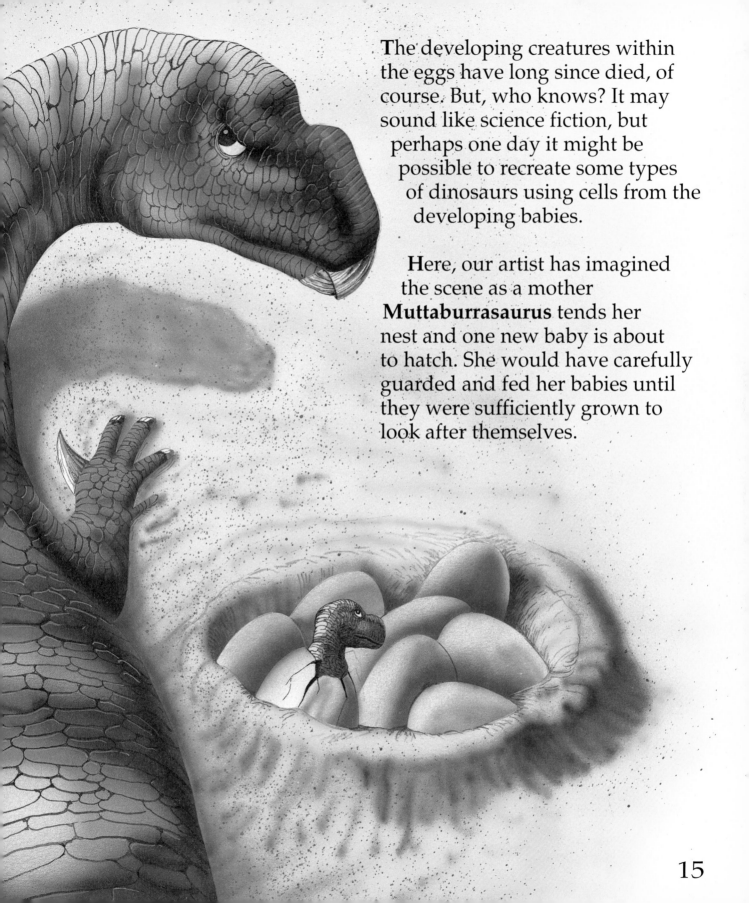

The developing creatures within the eggs have long since died, of course. But, who knows? It may sound like science fiction, but perhaps one day it might be possible to recreate some types of dinosaurs using cells from the developing babies.

Here, our artist has imagined the scene as a mother **Muttaburrasaurus** tends her nest and one new baby is about to hatch. She would have carefully guarded and fed her babies until they were sufficiently grown to look after themselves.

15

# Dinosaurs from down under

There have not been many dinosaur finds in Australia, but what skeletons have been discovered are very interesting to scientists. Most have been dug up recently, from the 1980s onward.

Quite a number of dinosaur tracks have also been discovered in Australia. In the state of Queensland, near a place called Winton, for example, scientists came across footprints that showed there had been a stampede of over one hundred dinosaurs in the area. No one knows why the stampede occurred. Most likely, however, an enormous carnivore had approached, so that smaller dinosaurs fled in panic. The tracks certainly show they ran off at great speed.

Apart from **Muttaburrasaurus**, other Cretaceous Australian dinosaurs include **Kakuru (1)**, a small, two-legged meat-eater whose name means "rainbow serpent." Scientists have only found remains of its legs so far, but from these bones they have calculated that it must have looked much like the picture below.

1

2

## Austrosaurus

(OST-ROW-SAW-RUS)
(**2**), meanwhile, was a long-necked, long-tailed, four-footed plant-eater about the length of two city buses. Its name means "southern lizard," and it is known for its long forelimbs.

**B**oth had to beware the awesome flesh-eater **Rapator** (RAP-A-TOR) (**3**), whose name means "plunderer."

**D**inosaur remains have also been found in New Zealand by the leading American paleontologist Ralph E. Molnar. An amateur fossil hunter, Joan Wiffen, has found some, too.

**D**inosaurs have been found in Antarctica, as well, under the ice that covers most of that polar region. This seems to show that Australia, New Zealand, and Antarctica were once part of a single, much larger landmass.

3

# If you find some

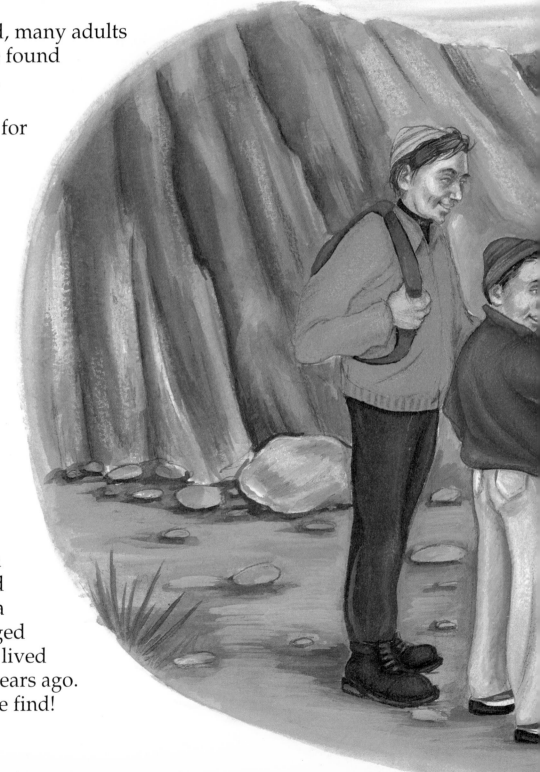

All over the world, many adults and children have found dinosaur remains.

In parts of China, for example, farmers have come across fossils in their fields. Not realizing what they were, some of these farmers have gone ahead and used some of the bones to build pigsties!

On the Isle of Wight, off the coast of southern England, in 1994, a six-year-old boy was lucky enough to spot a fossilized tooth and part of a skull. They belonged to a dinosaur that lived over 100 million years ago. What an incredible find!

18

# dinosaur bones . . .

So what do scientists recommend you do if you come across what might be dinosaur remains? Paleontologists are quick to point out that you should *not* try to move the pieces because you could easily damage them.

Instead, get in touch with the nearest natural history museum and tell them where you think you have spotted interesting remains. You might even qualify for a reward if they are rare!

Looking for dinosaur fossils can be fun, but never go fossil hunting alone. You need to have an adult with you, and, of course, you'll need permission to go on what may be private land.

# Muttaburrasaurus data

Scientists believe **Muttaburrasaurus** lived on Earth for 10 million years during Cretaceous times. It had a number of useful features that made it well suited to its surroundings.

## Broad head

**Muttaburrasaurus** had a low, broad head that ended in a sharp, horny beak. There was also a heavy, bony lump above its snout that would have protected it against a blow from an attacker. Like other members of its family, **Muttaburrasaurus** had no teeth at the front of its mouth, only at the side, in its cheeks. The beak was used to snip off plants and leaves, which the dinosaur would grind with its cheek teeth.

## Sharp hearing

Dinosaurs did not have ears on the sides of their heads. But this does not mean they could not hear. In fact, experts think they had a very good sense of hearing, with small holes at the sides of their heads to let in sound.

## Flexible neck

**Muttaburrasaurus** could move its neck easily to search for enemies making an approach.

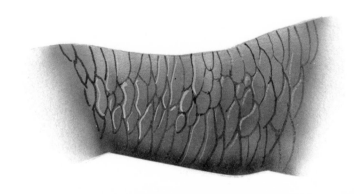

## Self-defense

If **Muttaburrasaurus** had to stay and fight, it was well equipped with its vicious thumb spikes. One jab with these would surely have sent any predator reeling away in pain, so that it would think twice before attacking again.

## Tapering tail

Broader at its base and narrower toward the tip, as you can see below, **Muttaburrasaurus**'s tail was held up off the ground when the dinosaur walked on all fours.

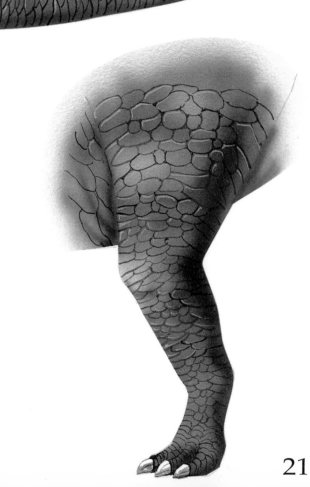

## Strong limbs

**Muttaburrasaurus** had four fingers on its front limbs that could be used for holding onto trees to help it when feeding, or for gripping an enemy. Its arms were flexible and could even be used to help **Muttaburrasaurus** walk on all fours. The back legs were very sturdy and solid, however, and helped support this dinosaur's weight.

21

# More like
# Muttaburrasaurus

**Muttaburrasaurus** (1) belonged to a family of plant-eating dinosaurs that lived all over the world during Cretaceous times. The members of this group are known as **Iguanodontids** (IG-WA-NO-DON-TIDS).

**Muttaburrasaurus** was very much like the biggest and best-known member of this family, **Iguanodon** (**2**). Remains of **Iguanodon** from Early Cretaceous times have been discovered in many countries, including England, Belgium, and Germany. It was a large creature, about 33 feet (10 m) long and over 16 feet (5 m) tall. It could have walked on two legs or on all fours. Its best-known features are its thumb spikes.

**A**nother member of the family was **Ouranosaurus** (OO-RAN -OH-SAW-RUS) (**3**). Found in the Sahara Desert in Niger, Africa, it was about 23 feet (7 m) long. As well as thumb spikes, it had a sail on its back that it used as a sort of heating and cooling system.

**Vectisaurus**, (VEK-TEE-SAW-RUS) (**4**) was a smaller relative, just 13 feet (4 m) long. This Early Cretaceous plant-eater was discovered on the Isle of Wight. Scientists think it might have had tall spines sticking up from its backbone. Very few of its bones have been found, however, and some scientists even think **Vectisaurus** was no more than a baby **Iguanodon**.

3

4

23

# GLOSSARY

**beak** — the hard outer part of a bird's or other animal's mouth; a bill.

**carnivores** — meat-eating animals.

**clutch** — a nest of eggs; a group of persons, animals, or objects gathered together.

**fossils** — traces or remains of plants and animals found in rock.

**herbivores** — plant-eating animals.

**paleontologists** — scientists who study the remains of plants and animals that lived millions of years ago.

**predators** — animals that kill other animals for food.

**remains** — a skeleton, bones, or dead body.

**reptiles** — cold-blooded animals that have hornlike or scale-covered skin.

**skeleton** — the bony framework of a body.

**snout** — protruding nose and jaw of an animal.

**spike** — long, thin, pointed object usually used to pierce or cut.

# INDEX